A Note to Parents

DK READERS is a compelling program for beginning readers, designed in conjunction with leading literacy experts, including Dr. Linda Gambrell, Distinguished Professor of Education at Clemson University. Dr. Gambrell has served as President of the National Reading Conference, the College Reading Association, and the International Reading Association.

Beautiful illustrations and superb full-color photographs combine with engaging, easy-to-read stories to offer a fresh approach to each subject in the series. Each DK READER is guaranteed to capture a child's interest while developing his or her reading skills, general knowledge, and love of reading.

The five levels of DK READERS are aimed at different reading abilities, enabling you to choose the books that are exactly right for your child:

Pre-level 1: Learning to read
Level 1: Beginning to read
Level 2: Beginning to read alone
Level 3: Reading alone
Level 4: Proficient readers

The "normal" age at which a child begins to read can be anywhere from three to eight years old. Adult participation through the lower levels is very helpful for providing encouragement, discussing storylines, and sounding out unfamiliar words.

No matter which level you select, you can be sure that you are helping your child learn to read, then read to learn!

DK

LONDON, NEW YORK, MUNICH,
MELBOURNE, AND DELHI

Editorial Assistant Ruth Amos
Senior Editor Elizabeth Dowsett
Senior Designer Lynne Moulding
Jacket Designer Lynne Moulding
Pre-production Producer Marc Staples
Producer Charlotte Oliver
Managing Editor Laura Gilbert
Design Manager Maxine Pedliham
Art Director Ron Stobbart
Publishing Director Simon Beecroft

Reading Consultant Dr. Linda Gambrell

Lucasfilm
Executive Editor J. W. Rinzler
Art Director Troy Alders
Keeper of the Holocron Leland Chee
Director of Publishing Carol Roeder

Rovio
Approvals Editor Nita Ukkonen
Senior Graphic Designer Jan Schulte-Tigges
Content Manager Laura Nevanlinna
Vice President of Book Publishing Sanna Lukander

First published in the United States in 2013
by DK Publishing
375 Hudson Street, New York, New York 10014
10 9 8 7 6 5 4 3 2 1

Page design copyright © 2013 Dorling Kindersley Limited

Angry Birds™ © 2009–2013 Rovio Entertainment Ltd.
All rights reserved.
© 2013 Lucasfilm Ltd. LLC & ® or TM where indicated.
All rights reserved. Used under authorization.

001–193695–June/13

DK books are available at special discounts when purchased in bulk
for sales promotions, premiums, fund-raising, or educational use.
For details, contact:
DK Publishing Special Markets
375 Hudson Street, New York, New York 10014
SpecialSales@dk.com

A catalog record for this book is available
from the Library of Congress.

ISBN: 978-1-4654-0188-5 (Paperback)
ISBN: 978-1-4654-0189-2 (Hardcover)

Color reproduction by Altaimage, UK
Printed and bound in the USA by Worzalla.

Discover more at
www.dk.com
www.starwars.com

Contents

DK READERS

BEGINNING
TO READ ALONE
2

ANGRY BIRDS™
STAR WARS®

LARD VADER'S VILLAINS

Written by Ruth Amos

The Pork Side

This is a very wicked
gang of pigs!
The pigs belong to the
Pig Empire and they
love to guzzle junk food.

Lard Vader

Emperor
Piglatine

The pigs are trying to find the legendary Egg, which holds the power to rule the galaxy.

First they must defeat the pesky Bird Rebels, who are defending the Bird Republic.

The birds want to be left in peace, but the pigs want power!

Boba Fatt

Pigtrooper

Guard

Lard Vader

Lard Vader is one of the
Pig Empire's chiefs.
His greatest ambition is to find
the mysterious Egg.

A long time ago he was a
Jedi, but then he joined the pigs.
The Jedi are warriors who serve
and protect the Bird Republic.

Lard Vader wants to be the most important pig, so he likes to stand on his Pigtrooper soldiers to seem taller. Unfortunately, he often falls off!

Pigtrooper

Another Pigtrooper!

Emperor Piglatine

Emperor Piglatine is the leader of the Pig Empire. He rules over all the other pigs in the galaxy.

Hidden weapon

The Emperor has banned all delicious junk food and candy in the galaxy, so that he can gobble it all down by himself.

Emperor Piglatine is not a very pretty pig—he has droopy green skin and a slimy snout. Luckily, the rest of his face is covered by a hood!

Lightsabers
The Emperor and his pigs fight with red lightsaber weapons. Bird Rebel warriors use blue ones.

The Emperor's guards

These guards are Emperor Piglatine's personal piggy protection They are supposed to follow behind the Emperor at all times to protect him.

Shiny visor

Silver forks
These are excellent for shoveling up as much food as possible!

Unfortunately, they are too busy tripping over one another's long robes to protect him!

The guards carry forks to help them deliver junk food and candy to their greedy leader.

Duel for piggy power

Emperor Piglatine has no idea that Lard Vader wants to be the leader of the pigs. Porky Piglatine is too busy eating as much food as possible to notice.

Button to turn
on lightsaber

Lard Vader often tries
to sneak up on the Emperor
with his lightsaber.
The Emperor thinks it is a
silly joke and just laughs at him!
Vader still hopes to be top pig.

Pigtroopers

Attention! This squadron of Pigtroopers are Emperor Piglatine's soldiers.
The Pigtroopers must search the galaxy for junk food and bring it back to the Emperor.

Triangle-shaped snout

Unfortunately, these soldier swine are utterly useless at their job—they often get lost. They hate asking for directions and they are not very good at using their snouts to sniff out clues.

Hard helmet

The Bird Rebels

Squawk! Look who it is!
This fantastic flock is called
the Bird Rebels.
These heroic adventurers must
fight to save the galaxy from the
wicked pigs.

Chuck
"Ham"
Solo

Terebacca

Red
Skywalker

Brilliant blaster

Ham keeps his blaster weapon in its holster at his side.

Lard Vader and his villainous friends keep trying to defeat the birds, but they are too brave and clever!

C-3PYOLK

R2-EGG2

Obi-Wan Kaboomi

Princess Stella Organa

Yoda Bird

The Pig Star

Behold, the Pig Star! The Pig Empire has built an incredible new super weapon, which has the power to blow up the entire universe!

The Pig Star has big ears and a round snout, just like the pigs.

The Bird Rebels are terrified
by the Pig Star's ferocious face—
even Princess Stella.

Jabba and bounty hunters

Monstrous Jabba the Hog is a wicked crime lord who secretly sells junk food. He often buys candy from the food smuggler and Bird Rebel, Ham Solo.

Jabba the Hog

Slug-like tail

Jabba likes to work with
other sneaky crooks.
He pays bounty hunter pigs to
track down birds who have escaped,
in exchange for a big sack of treats.
This bounty hunter has bulging
eyes for spotting runaway birds!

Bounty
hunter

Boba Fatt

Boba Fatt is another bounty hunter. Lard Vader pays Boba to zoom around the galaxy on his jetpack and find the *Mighty Falcon.*

Antenna for receiving messages

Jetpack
Boba's bright blue-and-orange jetpack propels him through space on his missions.

The *Falcon* is Ham Solo's fantastic starship.

Ham gives the Bird Rebels a ride in it when they go on quests.

Boba tries to stop the *Falcon*.

He wants to take the birds back to Lard Vader, who will give him lots of candy to slurp!

Imperial army

Lard Vader has different kinds
of pigs to fight for the Empire.
The pigs in white helmets are
called Snowtroopers, and they
wear special masks to shield
their snouts from the cold.

Pig Pilot

Pig Empire symbol

The Pig Pilots who wear black armor are in charge of zooming around the galaxy in aircraft. The Pig Commanders in white have red Pig Empire symbols on their helmets, and they give out silly orders to the Pigtroopers.

The Egg

This is The Egg that Lard Vader and his villains want! The Egg contains the Force— a form of energy that has the power to rule the universe. Yoda Bird disguised The Egg as the bird droid, R2-EGG2, to keep it safe.

Yoda Bird, Red Skywalker, and Obi-Wan Kaboomi are Jedi warriors, who study the Force to defend the Bird Republic. Red and Obi-Wan use thc Force to try to find The Egg. Unfortunately, old Yoda Bird keeps forgetting to tell the other Jedi where he hid it!

TIE fighter

Villainous vehicles

The wicked Pig Pilots have plenty of vehicles they use to carry out their pig patrols. The pigs fly TIE fighter aircraft with bulging eyes and big grins.

Wicked wings

Lard Vader has his own
fast, personalized TIE fighter
with glowing red eyes.
He expects all the other
TIE fighters to move out
of the way for him!

Breathing tubes
The Pig Pilots' masks
have special breathing
equipment to help
them breathe in space.

Big battle

On the frozen planet of Hoth, Lard Vader's villains ambush the Bird Rebels! The Pig Commanders ride huge AT-AT walkers across the snow. Luckily, the Bird Rebels defend themselves fiercely.

Red strikes with his lightsaber
and Ham Solo fires his blaster.

Victory to the Bird Rebels!
Lard Vader and the Pig Empire
must try again
another day . . .

AT-AT
walker

Quiz

1. Who is the leader of the Pig Empire?

2. What is the name of this vehicle?

3. Whose side is Red Skywalker on?

4. What is this super weapon called?

5. Where is The Egg hidden?